ECROW

Written and illustrated by

Valerie Littlewood

Julia MacRae Books

LONDON SYDNEY AUCKLAND JOHANNESBURG

First published in Great Britain 1992 by Julia MacRae, an imprint of the Random Century Group, 20 Vauxhall Bridge Road, London SW1V 2SA

Random Century Australia (Pty) Ltd, 20 Alfred Street, Milsons Point, Sydney, NSW 2061; Random Century New Zealand Ltd, PO Box 40-086, Glenfield, Auckland 10, New Zealand; Random Century South Africa (Pty) Ltd, PO Box 337, Bergvlei, 2012, South Africa
Printed in Hong Kong. British Library Cataloguing in Publication Data is available. ISBN 1-85681-022-4

ACKNOWLEDGEMENTS

I would like to thank the following for their help and support in the preparation of this book: The staff of the M.A. Course in Narrative Illustration and Editorial Design at Brighton Polytechnic, particularly George, Chris and John; John Key of Laughton for his farming advice; Norman Joplin for his help regarding model farm scarecrows; Keith Stewart of Stewkie Ltd; *The Farmer's Weekly*; Reading University Institute of Agricultural History; the relatives and friends who kept me well supplied with photographs, sketches and descriptions of scarecrows from all over the country; all the farmers, gardeners and enthusiasts whose creation and recording of scarecrows has made this book possible . . .
and a special thanks to Alan whose encouragement was constant and much appreciated.

BIBLIOGRAPHY

Many books and magazines, old and new, were consulted while researching this book, but the main sources of information were: *The Scarecrow, Fact and Fiction* by Peter Haining (Robert Hale, 1988); *The Scarecrow Book* by James Giblin and Dale Ferguson (Crown Publishing, N.Y., 1980); *British Toy Figures* by Norman Joplin (Arms and Armour Press, 1987); *The Standard Cyclopedia of Modern Agriculture* by Prof. Patrick Wright (Gresham, 1909); and *Farm Tools Through the Ages* by Michael Partridge (Osprey, 1973).

SCAR

CONTENTS

THE SCARECROW

When driving through the countryside you may glimpse a distant figure walking across the fields and dismiss it as a farm worker inspecting the crops. Only when you retrace your route and see the same figure in the same place will you recognise a scarecrow!

Scarecrow, mawkin, Jack-of-straw, scarehead, craw-deil, tattybogle or shoy-hoy, call him what you will, this strange figure has been used to protect precious food crops for over three thousand years and is still an important member of the farming community today.

Since Egyptian times the scarecrow has been recorded in paintings, poems, plays and prose. He is a sinister figure in myth, legend and the twentieth-century horror story, a rural curiosity in accounts of countryside life and ways, and a charming and much loved character in children's fiction.

Many bird-scaring devices have been tried over the years and though there is some doubt about the effectiveness of the traditional scarecrow, in this celebration we will see that he is still 'alive' and well, a friend to children, an ally to farmers, and always helping in the fight against that age-old adversary – the bird.

10

BEASTLY BIRDS

Rooks, pigeons, starlings, sparrows, finches, geese ... the list goes on and on. It must have seemed to the first farmers that all the birds of the air had been sent at one season or another to snatch the grain or nibble at the new growth.

Despite modern scaring devices, birds still delight in a free meal. They watch from a safe distance until all is quiet, and then fly down, each to its favourite food; pigeons to cabbage, rooks to new corn, sparrows to the wheat and finches to fruit buds.

One bird which the misnamed 'scarecrow' need not discourage is the crow himself, a much maligned bird who prefers a solitary meal of grubs and carrion to the noisy activities of his relative the rook. Marauding rooks are sometimes shot, and their bodies hung from sticks as a warning to other birds. But the birds are not entirely bad. They also clear the ground of harmful grubs and small pests so farmers are usually content to frighten them away rather than resort to the gun.

The traditional scarecrow is certainly a deterrent, but when the birds learn that he is powerless, they treat him with contempt, cheekily pecking around his feet and, as a final insult, stealing shreds of his stuffing to furnish the nests of future seed snatchers.

CLAPPERS & CALLERS

The scarecrow we are most familiar with today is the silent stationary figure, set in the middle of a field, but the first and at one time the most common scarecrow was very much alive.

Early British records show that it was usually the job of small boys, or men too old for strenuous farm tasks, to go out into the fields with wooden rattles or clappers to scare the birds.

They spent hours in all weathers, wielding heavy clappers, throwing stones and shouting. With only rough shelters of sticks and mud to protect them from the rain and wind, they sang songs and recited rhymes to keep their spirits up as they worked.

Small boys not only protected field crops. In Elizabethan times they were also employed to run up and down orchards, frightening greedy birds from cherry trees.

Perhaps for the older men, a day in the field as a human scarecrow was a welcome rest from ploughing or sowing but the loneliness and cold must have been hard, especially for the young scarecrows, their day-long vigils often supplemented with other tasks such as weeding, hoeing, or stone-clearing.

Economics make it almost impossible to employ a human scarecrow today, but he would surely still be the most effective deterrent. It is obviously the combination of human presence and unexpected, sudden movement that ruffles thieving feathers most.

MEN OF STRAW

There are as many different scarecrows as there are farmers to make them. Each is an individual in dress, attitude and effectiveness!

All have their own character. Some stand with arms and legs stiff and straight. Others flap loosely – one may be striding out across the land waving a flag, another will protect fish from herons by a pool. Gruesome scarecrows

hang from makeshift gibbets, or are hoisted up on poles to swing in the wind.

Their faces may be happy, sad, blank, or sinister. They sport scarves, hats, possibly a pair of goggles or sun glasses. Some have socks for hands, or gloves for ears, and others are dressed in curious mixtures of skirts, trousers, blouses and waistcoats. They carry a great variety of weapons: streamers, tin cans, bits of flapping cloth, flags, sticks and foil lids.

Some scarecrows are the result of patient care and are very lifelike, while others are just rags and sticks hastily erected. But whatever their standard of dress or construction, these bizarre farm hands are never found shirking their tasks.

16

FIELD DUTY

Through rain, wind, snow, sleet and blazing sun, the scarecrow will stay at his post, guarding the crops all year round from sowing to harvest. In the spring they protect young corn and new growth of oilseed rape; in the summer, they frighten away pigeons from peas and cabbages; and in the autumn and winter they keep cold and lonely vigil over early sowings of wheat and rape.

The traditional scarecrow is the most often seen deterrent in the field, but the protection of extremely valuable crops brings out the inventor in the farming community. There are now inflatable plastic scarecrows which can be dressed to the farmer's taste, flags with huge eyes painted on them, pvc silhouettes of shooting scarecrows, humming tapes, gas-guns, and a wonderful self-inflating scarecrow who not only leaps up, emitting a loud shriek, but also glows in the dark!

The most effective scarer seems to be a huge hawk-shaped kite which ranges across the field on wires, casting the ominous shadow of a bird of prey. Sometimes the old and new are combined when a straw man is placed sitting next to the noisy gas-gun whose irregular explosions make it the most disliked of all bird scaring devices – turning the quiet fields into battlefields as the war against the birds continues.

STRIPES & STREAMERS

A popular feature in towns and cities is the allotment garden, an area of land which has been sub-divided into small plots, each tended by a different tenant. Here the scarecrow can be seen in his most urban environment.

An allotment is defined as a piece of land of 300 square yards. In the past, allotments were provided by country landlords to enable their tenants to supplement income and food.

During the war years and in times of depression, allotments played a vital part in feeding the family, especially in city areas where few people had gardens.

Today there are fewer allotments, but now they have become the home of the prize vegetable. At the height of the growing season these small areas of land are festooned with an array of bird scaring devices.

The traditional scarecrow is aided by tapes, nets, flags, tin cans and old wheel hubs, anything that flutters, sparkles, or rattles, to keep the thieving birds away from the produce.

Sometimes criticized as scruffy and defying attempts to regulate the huts and sheds, the allotment garden remains a lively if haphazard tribute to local gardeners and their scarecrows. The allotment scarecrow is more personalised, perhaps reflecting the character of the tenant.

GARDEN GHOSTS

The most intimate home of the scarecrow must be the garden. Here he becomes a family friend, protecting even the smallest rows of peas and beans, fruits and cabbages.

In the garden, pest control is carried out on the most detailed scale. Great time and care are taken in threading foil onto string, hanging long thin strips of plastic on sticks and stringing cotton over new shoots. Fruit bushes are adorned with old net curtains, and old wives' lore employed to keep away the smallest pests.

Moles are discouraged by sinking a bottle into the ground with the neck poking out so that the wind makes an eerie wailing sound down the runs. Slugs are trapped under leaves with fruit bait and drown intoxicated in jars of beer.

Pigeons are frightened away by painting an upturned bottle red. Mice are kept from pea seeds by putting holly in the trenches! And even the farmer's dead crow is imitated by sticking feathers in a potato and suspending it from a stick.

At night the vegetable plot is besieged by pests and so the scarecrow is aided by the addition of mirrors and tin lids, which glimmer in the light from windows and street lamps. Scare-cat heads with sparkling marble eyes are hung from posts to frighten away mice. Inflatable plastic owls peer down from fruit trees where, during daylight, they keep small birds from the crop.

All this, with the wailing of the mole scarer, makes a walk in the night garden a spooky experience.

FARMYARD & FANCY DRESS

I n the child's world the scarecrow is a regular and popular character, thanks to the two most famous fictional scarecrows – Worzel Gummidge, the scarecrow from Scatterbrook Farm, created by Barbara Euphan Todd, and the scarecrow without a brain from Frank Baum's *The Wizard of Oz*. These much loved characters give an insight into the scarecrow's view of life; both were based on scarecrows seen near the authors' respective English and American homes.

The success of these characters through the media of book, radio, television and film, has earned the scarecrow a lasting part in the child's world of make-believe.

Any fancy-dress competition, especially in rural areas, is bound to bring a crop of scarecrows, sprouting straw from ancient hats and outworn jackets with cut-out crows and carrot-shaped noses – all imitating their fictional heroes.

There have been scarecrow puppets, scarecrow dolls and models, but perhaps the most enduring toy scarecrows belong to the model farms.

Originally, these were lead figures, and a set contained all a child needed to create a miniature working farm. Livestock, corn stooks, milk churns the farmer, his wife, milkmaid, cowman, hedging and gates... and of course the scarecrow. The farms were introduced after the First World War when manufacturers found a decline in the sale of toy soldiers and created the 'home farm' as a replacement.

The lead version was later replaced with more practical plastic and non-toxic figures, and these are still sold as components of the model farm today.

MYTHS
& MAGIC

Far away from the cosy children's scarecrow is the character of folklore and the 20th-century horror story.

Scarecrows have been brought to life by magic, used as disguises for spies, look-outs and murderers; dead bodies are hidden in them and they are hosts to ghosts and spirits. At magic festivals such as Hallowe'en, they come alive, spiriting away children and dragging their victims down into the soil.

The Greek scarecrow figure has its

origins in the myth of the god Priapus, which tells how the ugly baby of Dionysus and Aphrodite was adopted by vineyard keepers who saw that birds feasting on the grapes were frightened away by the boy's ugly face and body.

When news spread of this unwitting scarecrow, other farmers carved wooden statues resembling Priapus and stood them in their fields hoping for the same effect. Since then Priapus has become the god of gardens, and is often depicted with a club for protection and a sickle to encourage a good harvest.

There can be an uneasy feeling accompanying the sudden sighting of a scarecrow, a pricking of the hairs on the back of the neck at being watched by those unseeing eyes, or a sudden shock at stumbling over the boot of a discarded scarecrow lying at the edge of a field.

Sometimes you may wonder who is watching who?

STRANGE SIGHTINGS

In addition to his agricultural or domestic habitat, men of straw turn up in some unexpected places: resting between seasons in the barn, protecting fish from herons at a local pond, posted guard at the farm gate, lurking discarded in a ditch, or hoisted up into a tree out of the way of farm machinery.

In the farmyard waiting to be taken to the field, he becomes an impromptu 'Aunt Sally' for the children to throw stones at, and in the winter he's a lonely snowman in the field.

Some scarecrows defy convention and in true 'make-do' fashion are constructed from odd materials. Giant corrugated iron figures tower over early wheat with spinners for heads. Sheets of plastic are twisted into a rough shape, and even an old suit of armour was seen earlier this century, combining all the best attributes of a scarecrow in a shiny noisy figure.

Guy Fawkes night unfortunately brings some old scarecrows to the end of their lives. Raised up to the top of the bonfire they become 'the guy' to be burned amidst a shower of fireworks and celebrations. Perhaps this is quite a fitting end for a scarecrow. He goes out in a blaze of glory celebrating the harvest and looking forward to a new season and new scarecrows!

MAKING A SCARECROW

Take two strong sticks and nail one across the other to form the skeleton.
Stuff an old boiler suit with straw and tie it to the stake with twine or rope. For the head, use anything: an old sack, a plastic bag. Paint a face on it, or add a mask.
Push the head well on to the stake and tie firmly.

~

Now you have your basic scarecrow, you can add any details you like: jackets, coats, dresses – a hat, gloves, scarf, perhaps some worn-out wellington boots.
You will need something to flap, so add some fluttering plastic streamers, create some noise with pebbles in a tin can suspended from his hand.
To make him look busy, give him a stick to shake or a flag to wave.

~

Position him to stride out across the field and dig him in well, secure against all inclement weathers, and as a final touch perhaps give him a companion – a cut-out dog.
Stand back and admire your handiwork and see how many friends wave a greeting to the familiar coat (and how few birds take any notice!).

TIN CAN

TWINE

STONES TO RATTLE!

OLD OVERALLS

JACKET

STICK FOR FLAGS

OLD BOOTS

WHITE PLASTIC BAG

PAINTS

2 STRONG STICKS

HAT

SCARF

GLOVES

STRAW FOR STUFFING

PLYWOOD FOR DOG

PLASTIC FOR FLAG

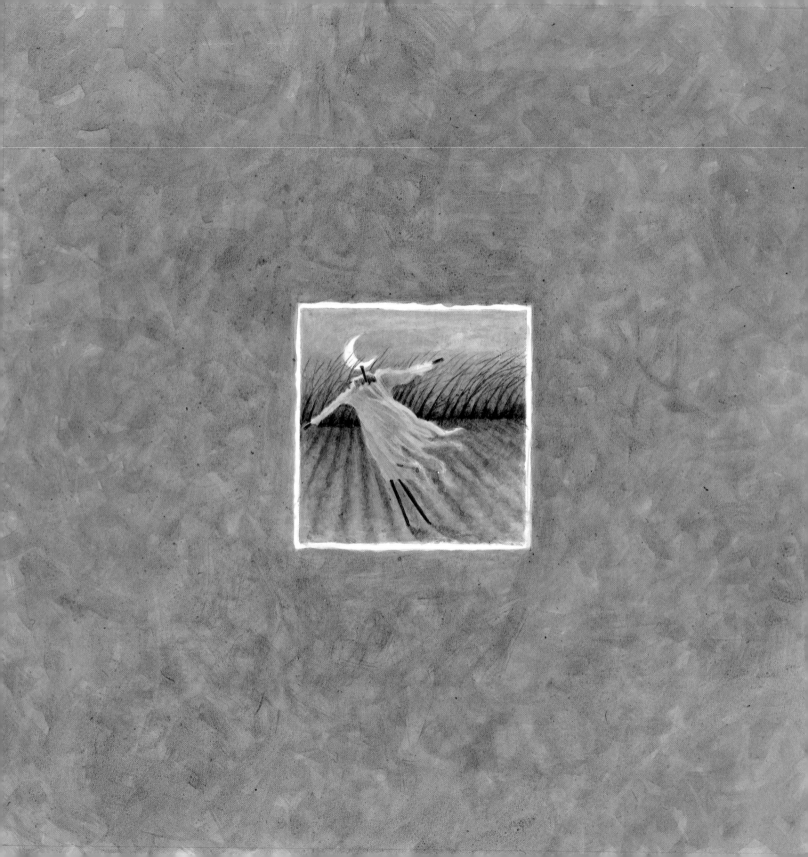